Original title:
Roots of Solitude

Copyright © 2025 Creative Arts Management OÜ
All rights reserved.

Author: Benjamin Caldwell
ISBN HARDBACK: 978-1-80581-943-1
ISBN PAPERBACK: 978-1-80581-470-2
ISBN EBOOK: 978-1-80581-943-1

Whispers in the Stillness

In the quiet, cats take naps,
Squirrels plotting little mishaps.
A mouse in a cheese shop sings,
Dodging boots and other things.

The snail takes a leisurely stroll,
On a leaf, he makes his goal.
Gossip floats on breezy air,
While frogs croak without a care.

Echoes Beneath the Surface

Bubbles rise from a fishy chat,
About the world outside the mat.
A goldfish dreams of ancient seas,
Where mermaids giggle with the breeze.

Crabs dance on tiny little feet,
While octopuses keep the beat.
Clams whisper secrets in the sand,
Wishing one day to form a band.

Solitary Shadows at Dusk

The shadows stretch and have a ball,
Their silly shapes amuse us all.
A tree thinks it's a giant's hat,
While a squirrel laughs at a sleeping bat.

The streetlamp flickers with delight,
Telling jokes to bugs at night.
While wisps of clouds float by in glee,
Arguing if they're better than me.

Deep Waters of the Mind

In the depths where thoughts reside,
A fish wears glasses, looks quite spry.
Swimmers practice their best dive,
While dreaming of a turkey twerkin' jive.

A jellyfish tickles a weary brain,
Sharing jokes in the underwater lane.
A whirlpool swirls with laughter grand,
As ideas drift like grains of sand.

Beneath the Surface Stillness

In a pond where frogs just sit,
Ducks quack jokes, they think they're it.
Turtles surf on lily pads,
While fish gossip, oh it's mad!

The water's calm, a grand charade,
Yet laughter lurks beneath the shade.
Who knew the depths held such a jest?
A fishy party, who's the best?

Embrace of the Unseen

Here in shadows, we all play,
Invisible friends come out to sway.
A tickle from the ghostly breeze,
Makes me laugh, oh what a tease!

Cupboards creak with hidden cheer,
A sock's lost but never fear.
There's joy in what we cannot see,
Like squirrels that dance, feeling free.

Hidden Depths of Solitude

In a cupboard stacked with dusty shoes,
Haunted hats sing the blues.
They reminisce about the flair,
Of dancing feet that once were there.

Among the cobwebs, laughter lingers,
Tickling corners with unseen fingers.
The dust bunnies chuckle in delight,
As they prance through the moonlit night.

Solace in the Forgotten Corners

Under the bed, a sock parade,
With mismatched pairs, a wacky trade.
Each corner holds a secret plot,
With treasures that might hit the spot.

Old toys laugh and share their tales,
Of pirate ships and paper sails.
In dusty nooks, they find their fun,
While shadows wait for the morning sun.

The Silence Between the Stars

In the dark, where silence creeps,
Even the moon has lost her peeps.
Stars are laughing, what a show,
Echoes of giggles in the glow.

Comets zoom with a playful grin,
Winking at planets where they've been.
Galaxies swirl in a dance so sly,
While silence hums a lullaby.

Aliens play hide-and-seek at night,
With a wink, they take their flight.
In the corner of the cosmic scene,
You'd swear they're playing, unseen.

So next time you gaze at the sky,
Remember the jokes as you sigh.
Between the stars, a jest awaits,
In that silence, the cosmos debates.

Beneath the Bark of Time

Inside the tree, where whispers dwell,
Bark is thick like a funny shell.
Squirrels gossip, acorns drop,
Time rolls by, will it ever stop?

Mice are plotting with a soft squeak,
While shadows chuckle, play hide and seek.
Rabbits lounge, sipping dew,
How do they know just what to do?

Fungi dance in a top hat's flair,
Cheering on the beetles who dare.
Nature laughs, it's quite a show,
Underneath where the whispers grow.

So next you spy a gnarled tree,
Think of the jokes conversed with glee.
Beneath the bark, oh what a rhyme,
Life's punchline hides in the seams of time.

Hidden Depths of Isolation

In the corner, where shadows blend,
Isolation's got a funny friend.
Dust bunnies chuckle in huddled clumps,
Rats tell tales of their mystic jumps.

In the quiet, whispers plot schemes,
Frogs in pajamas host wild dreams.
A cactus cracks a prickly joke,
While the lonely old chair starts to poke.

Under the bed, a monster's shy,
Hiding from sunlight, oh my!
He trips on sneakers, and what a sight,
His laugh echoes deep into the night.

So if you feel a little alone,
Remember laughter connects like a bone.
In hidden depths, the humor flows,
With friends you never knew, oh how it grows.

A Single Leaf in Autumn

One leaf trembles on a branch so high,
With a funny wiggle, it bids goodbye.
The wind cracks jokes, trying to tease,
As the leaf sways in the autumn breeze.

All its friends have made their fall,
But this one leaf is having a ball.
It spins around, a solo dance,
Grabbing attention with its glance.

Down below, squirrels start to cheer,
For the bravest leaf, the star of the year!
"Go on, drop down!" the crowd all shouts,
While the leaf just laughs, twisting about.

So if you see it floating down,
Remember its giggles, not a frown.
A single leaf with all the flair,
In autumn's cloak, a humor rare.

Footprints in the Absence

In the garden where no one roams,
My shadows dance and call me home.
The squirrels gossip, the leaves just sigh,
I talk to myself like a passerby.

The birds are busy, but not in flight,
They sit and giggle, what a sight!
I trip on dreams, they roll by fast,
And wonder how long this day will last.

With every echo that makes me grin,
I count my quirks, where to begin?
These footprints lead to nowhere near,
Just me and my laughter, loud and clear.

The Gallery of Unshared Dreams

In a space where wishes paint the wall,
A canvas made for one, after all.
Each brushstroke whispers, 'Just me here,'
With colors that twirl like a playful deer.

The frames are empty, yet full of cheer,
Framed giggles echo; do you hear?
A masterpiece of silly scenes,
With dandelion fluff and jellybeans!

A solo exhibit of whimsical sights,
Where zaftig winks take frequent flights.
I'd share with you, but who has time?
This gallery's mine — it's quite sublime!

Whispers in the Gloom

Beneath the blanket of evening's shade,
The chairs giggle where dreams are laid.
Sock puppets gossip overheard,
While the dust bunnies dance, absurd!

Ghosts of laughter float in the air,
Reminiscing moments that seemed quite rare.
In the corners, secrets tumble and zoom,
Here's a riddle — why is silence a room?

A ticklish breeze plays hide-and-seek,
In the stillness, whispers softly speak.
They share the tale of the night so bright,
Making solitude feel just right.

Anchors of Silence

In a boat of thoughts, I drift away,
With oars made from dreams, I laugh and play.
The waves chuckle; they tease and twirl,
As my anchor snoozes, what a swirl!

This ocean screams with quiet delight,
While fish wear hats, what a silly sight!
Deep dives in laughter, floating like foam,
Who knew solitude could feel like home?

I cast my net, but it catches air,
As my bubbles bounce, I stop and stare.
The silence hums a playful tune,
Guiding my boat by the light of the moon.

The Lonesome Whisper

In a room full of echoes, I talk to my cat,
She nods with approval, as I wear my hat.
We debate about snacks, and who's the real boss,
She claims it's the tuna, I argue it's sauce.

Curled in my blanket, I share all my fears,
The walls bring me comfort, no judgment appears.
They creak and they whisper like friends made of wood,
No one disturbs us, and that's pretty good.

Solitude's Gentle Embrace

My couch is a throne for a king made of snacks,
With a scepter of chips, I plot my attacks.
The popcorn brigade stands ready to fight,
While I rule my domain, in this glorious night.

I laugh at my shadow, it's good company,
We dance in the twilight, just my cat and me.
Oh, the joy of my kingdom, no taxes to pay,
In pajamas as armor, I conquer the day.

A Meadow of Unsaid Words

Conversations with pillows, how silly it seems,
They listen with patience, fulfilling my dreams.
I ponder profound thoughts, like toast vs. the jam,
And whether those socks match, I question my plan.

The ceiling's my canvas, my thoughts start to roam,
Imaginary friends gather round my home.
We giggle 'bout nothing, as laughter takes flight,
In this meadow of whispers, we're all out of sight.

The Echo Chamber of One

In the echo chamber, I'm quite the big shot,
With a voice that can make all my jokes hit the spot.
The mirror cracks up, with applause so sincere,
Thank you, dear audience, I'll see you next year!

I juggle my daydreams, they laugh 'til they cry,
Sometimes I join in, a real stand-up guy.
With a punchline or two, I'm fluffing my nest,
In this echo of one, I'm truly the best!

Echoes of Distant Shadows

In a room with a cat and a sock,
I pondered time's tick-tock.
The shadows dance, they laugh and play,
While I whisper secrets to a stray.

The fridge hums a lively tune,
As I debate with my spoon.
Each echo brings a chuckle near,
My solo dance with ice-cold beer.

I once tried to bake a cake,
But ended up with a pancake.
Who needs friends when flour's a friend?
Just me and my whisk, this trend won't end.

With socks mismatched, I roam the hall,
Questioning if this is fun at all.
A laugh escapes, I trip on air,
In my kingdom of one, without a care.

Solitary Reflections

A mirror shows my best side yet,
But it's hard to find where I've met.
These conversations with my potted plant,
Make me wonder if I've lost my slant.

Sipping tea with a gnome so spry,
He tells me tales without a sigh.
Each chuckle echoes through the day,
As I contemplate my own cabaret.

The couch whispers sweet nothings to me,
Suggesting a nap; it's offering tea.
I giggle, friends have tried to intrude,
But I've decided solitude's my mood.

With socks that mismatch in splendid delight,
I dance through the day like a quirky sight.
Can a life be funny and yet so plain?
I guess it's the laughter that keeps me sane.

The Quiet Path Within

There's a path inside my cluttered mind,
Filled with thoughts, interesting yet blind.
I stroll along with a pen in hand,
Jotting down jokes—like a humor band.

Tea brewed strong, I sit by the wall,
Imagining debates with a rubber doll.
We laugh about wearing hats and scarves,
Inventing the rules of the lonely narves.

I once tried to be a flower in bloom,
But tripped on my roots and fell in my room.
Laughter echoes off the walls of my mind,
Who knew solitude could be so much fun to find?

With each misstep, I dance with flair,
In my heart, there's light; I shed despair.
Thus I walk this quiet bumpy lane,
Finding joy, even when it's mundane.

Unraveled Threads of Self

My thoughts are tangled like old yarn,
Spinning stories of wonder and charm.
Each thread unravels, creating a mess,
Yet solitude's laughter feels like a bless.

I tried to knit a scarf; what a sight!
The wool's now a creature with no bite.
It giggles at me from the floor,
Saying, 'You might as well knit something more.'

Chasing dust bunnies, I find a sock,
And name it Gregory, it's anti-clock.
Together we lounge in the softest of grace,
Who needs company? We've got this space!

So here we are, with laughs that ensue,
A sock, a bunny, and thoughts to construe.
In a world where I rule—no one to tell,
I'm the star of my show, and I'm doing swell!

A Flicker in the Solitary Grove

In a grove where squirrels chatter,
A lone tree dreams of flying.
It wears a hat made of old leaves,
And claims the sun is just shy, oh my!

The branches sway in awkward glee,
As they try to dance with bees.
But the bees, they laugh and tease,
'You can't grow wings, so take it easy!'

A toad hops by, with a grin so wide,
He juggles acorns, full of pride.
'Life's a circus,' he croaks with cheer,
'Just keep it weird, and don't fear the weird!'

So in this grove, they play all day,
All creatures in their own quirky way.
A flicker of joy, a spark of fun,
In this solitary space, they've won!

Where Shadows Wander Alone

In the park where shadows meet,
One likes to dance, the other, retreat.
They argue softly, who's got the flair,
But they both just linger, not going anywhere.

One shadow wears a silly hat,
The other says, 'You look like a nat!'
Together they bicker and play charades,
While the moon giggles, as daylight fades.

They play hopscotch, on pavement cracks,
Stumbling and falling, no one keeps tracks.
'You lead today,' a shadow softly grins,
But you know they'll swap when the next round begins.

So there they sit, in a whirling dance,
Two shadows twisting, lost in their chance.
Finding laughter where light bends low,
In a world where funny shadows glow.

The Canvas of a Lone Heart

A singular heart paints with glee,
Splashing colors on a canvas wild and free.
It trips on hues of blue and red,
Then chuckles softly, 'Oh, where's my head?'

The brushes dance, oh what a sight,
'Let's do polka dots, make it bright!'
Yet every attempt is a quirky fail,
Creating art that tells a odd tale.

It splatters green where orange should be,
A masterpiece of pure absurdity.
With a wink, it says, 'A masterpiece born!'
And the paintbrush giggles, 'What have we sworn?'

So in this art where laughter blooms,
A lone heart giggles in technicolor rooms.
Each stroke a pun, each splatter a cheer,
In the wild expanse of a world so dear.

In the Company of Thorns

In a garden sprouting spiky cheer,
Thorns sit together, full of sneer.
'You're prickly,' one says with a laugh,
'And you're sharp but still full of half!'

They try to hug with poky arms,
But end up tangling in each other's charms.
'Next time, let's stick to just a wave,'
They giggle, in a thorny enclave.

With roses nearby, they watch in awe,
As blooms sway gently, with grace and flaw.
'Why can't we be as delicate as they?'
'Thorns aren't soft, but we surely can play!'

So they play tag, in their prickly way,
Laughing as petals flutter away.
In the company of edges so wild,
They find true joy, like a playful child.

Embracing the Silence

In the quiet of my room, I ponder,
My socks on strike, I watch them wander.
A pinball machine of thoughts takes flight,
I laugh when my lunch takes a bite!

The dog stares at me, quite confused,
Judging my snacks, feeling bemused.
With cereal curtains and milk for a door,
I toast to the peace, then drop on the floor.

The clock, it ticks, with sarcastic glee,
Mocking my solitude, hiding with me.
A dance with my shadows, a jig on the wall,
I twirl with the echoes, I'm having a ball!

So here in my fortress of calm and of cheer,
I search for the laughs, and sometimes a tear.
I embrace all the stillness, the giggles inside,
In the arms of the quiet, I take a wild ride!

Shadows of the Heart

In corners where dust bunnies dare not tread,
I find my old journals, like llamas in bed.
They whisper sweet nothings, like tales told by dreams,
I giggle and wonder if laughter redeems.

Shadows flicker, like they're planning a heist,
I offer them cookies, they've got quite the taste.
Oh, do they pause or just wait for a sign?
Together we snicker, I'll toast them with wine!

In the cocoon of my thoughts, silly things take flight,
Like socks in the dryer at the end of the night.
They flutter and dance, these phantoms of fun,
Making mischief in silence, with a giggle or pun.

So let them cavort in their jovial spree,
These shadows of heart, who come hang out with me.
In fits of distraction, we chuckle away,
Finding joy in the silence, come what may!

The Cradle of Self-Reflection

I nestle in cushions, like marshmallow fluff,
Contemplating life from my couch, oh so tough.
The cat's judging hard, with a paw on my face,
As I scratch my head, ruffled in place.

A mirror reflects all my quirky designs,
Each wrinkle and giggle, a laugh intertwined.
I try to look wise, but my hair has its say,
Reflecting like mirrors, it takes me away.

With snacks on the side, and a show on repeat,
I ponder my choices, till I hop to my feet.
There's wisdom in chips and proverbs in dips,
I embrace my reflections; they bring me sweet quips.

So here in my cradle of humorous thought,
I juggle my whims, with the wisdom I've sought.
For laughter is balm, and self-deprecation,
Turns solitude's corners into pure jubilation!

Treading Lightly on Shadows

I tiptoe through shadows, like they're made of silk,
Pondering life over a warm glass of milk.
"Excuse me," I say, as my feet start to prance,
These shadows are partners, in my lonely dance.

With giggles and whispers, they follow close by,
Sipping my tea, while they twinkle and sigh.
In hues of golden laughter, we jest and we play,
Pretending that life is a sweet cabaret.

From sofa to fridge, a comical chore,
My shadows keep up, always asking for more.
In this odd ballet, we'll prance and we'll spin,
Treading lightly on laughter, the only true win.

So here's to the shadows, my partners in jest,
Thankful for moments where silence feels blessed.
In the dance of the quiet, we twirl in delight,
Finding joy in the shadows that vanish from sight!

The Solitary Grove

In a grove where no one goes,
A squirrel chats with trees, who knows?
The branches sway and gently grin,
While shadows play a game of sin.

The owl hoots jokes that make no sense,
While crickets join in with a fence.
The wind whispers secrets quite absurd,
Even the stones have quite a word.

Dreaming in Isolation

In a corner, dreaming tight,
A mouse plays chess with a fly at night.
Each move they make is quite a mess,
Yet they laugh at their own distress.

The clock ticks slow as if on strike,
While shadows dance, oh what a hike!
The dreams they share are wildly loud,
Just me and my thoughts, oh how proud!

Sanctuary of the Mind

A castle built with thoughts so wild,
Imaginary dragons, my inner child.
The moat is deep with giggles deep,
And not a single soul to weep.

With clouds for pillows, I take a nap,
Unbothered by the world's great map.
The laughter echoes through the halls,
While imaginary knights make silly calls.

Unspoken Bonds of Loneliness

In my mind, I host a ball,
With no-one here, I stand so tall.
The shadows twirl in masquerade,
While I sip tea that dreams have made.

A parrot squawks, my only guest,
He tells me jokes, I laugh the best.
Together we share a quirky dance,
In this grand silence, we take a chance.

Celestial Whispers in the Dark

In shadows deep, I hear them tease,
The stars giggle as they float with ease.
A comet's tail whispers a silly joke,
While planets spin, enchanted and woke.

Moonbeams wink, they pull my leg,
Saying, 'Dance alone, just lose the peg!'
The night sky laughs, a cosmic jest,
Who knew solitude could be such a fest?

Alien chats in the vast unknown,
Floating around like they're not alone.
But here I stand, in my fuzzy socks,
While stardust bounces off my city blocks.

So let me twirl in this lonely space,
With a smile stretched wide upon my face.
I'll grab a star, and hold it tight,
For in the dark, I find my light.

Flickers of Hope in Silence

In quiet corners where shadows loom,
I trip on dreams with a playful boom.
A silence dances on tiptoes near,
Whispering wishes, always sincere.

An empty chair begs for company,
I sit and sip my imaginary tea.
The spoon sings softly—what a delight!
I converse with echoes into the night.

Lonely thoughts, like butterflies white,
Flutter around in a comical flight.
With every blink, they lose their poise,
Chasing my laughter, oh what a noise!

So here's to the chuckle in the hush,
Where giggles rise in a gentle rush.
I'll toast to the quiet that makes me grin,
In solitude's arms, I always win.

The Alchemy of Alone

In my lab of one, potions abound,
Mixing solitude's magic, quite profound.
A dash of whimsy, a cup of cheer,
Brewing up laughter like a fine souvenir.

Add a sprinkle of nonsense, let it bubble,
Stirring the cauldron of delightful trouble.
Giggling ghouls in the corner prance,
While I take my potion and join the dance.

Monsters of boredom, they all take flight,
Chasing joy like a mischievous sprite.
I bottle my giggles, let them grow,
For the alchemy of alone steals the show!

So here's to the potion of silly allure,
A patchwork of solitude, so pure.
I'll sip on my brew, and laugh some more,
In this quirky lab, there's never a bore!

Stillness in the Heart of Chaos

In the whirlwind, I find my groove,
Dancing over papers, making my move.
The mess surrounds like a wild parade,
Yet in the calm, my troubles fade.

Chaos cackles, a raucous delight,
While I juggle dreams with all of my might.
The clock ticks laughter, such funny tunes,
As I whirl through deadlines like playful loons.

In the middle of storms, I take a stand,
With a banana peel in my hand.
Milk spills, laughter fills up the air,
Who knew chaos could transform with care?

So let the winds of mayhem swirl,
I'll twirl like a dervish, give it a whirl.
For in the eye of the storm, I say,
Solitude shines in the most colorful way!

Illuminated by Solitude

In a room, I talk to my chair,
It listens well, shows no despair.
The walls are my company, so divine,
They echo my jokes, with perfect timing.

A sock on the floor, my dear friend,
We share secrets, 'til day's end.
My cat judges me with a dignified stare,
I wonder if she's got a better career.

Juggling my thoughts like balloons in air,
I trip on my dreams, it's quite the affair.
Cup of tea spills, now a mess at my feet,
But my inner circus feels so complete.

So here I sit, with my thoughts all a-jumble,
Life gets funnier when I choose to fumble.
Embracing the chaos, with laughter and cheers,
In the spotlight of laughter, my heart disappears.

The Sigh of the World Unnoticed

The clock tick-tocks in a rhythm so funny,
While I miss the chime and my tea turns runny.
Street lamps blink, as if sharing a joke,
I chuckle alone, while the world just stokes.

The mailman waves with a puzzled frown,
I reply with a smile, but I'm wearing a gown.
Postcards from places I never will see,
I send them to myself, from the land of 'me'.

Dancing dust bunnies in the afternoon light,
They twirl and caper, what a glorious sight!
I join their ballet, though I've two left feet,
We laugh 'til we're dizzy and call it a treat.

So here's to the world that's busy and grand,
While I sit alone, with my socks unplanned.
A sigh for the hustle, a chuckle for me,
In my quiet domain, I'm as happy as can be.

The Art of Embracing Nothingness

Sitting in silence, I find it quite bold,
My thoughts on a journey, they're artfully told.
With snacks in my lap, I ponder the great,
The meaning of nothing, oh what a fate!

A spoonful of boredom, a dash of regret,
I whip up a smoothie of 'what did I forget?'
The fridge hums a tune, it's quite the duet,
As I sip on my dreams and await my next set.

I talk to my plants, their wisdom is grand,
They nod and they sway; the best of the band.
In the silence I find my most humorous muse,
Nothingness brings joy, who needs the blues?

So here's to the art of finding a thrill,
In moments of nothing, I get my fill.
A canvas of laughter, a palette of peace,
Embracing the void, where absurdities cease.

The Silent Chronicles of a Heart

My heart writes tales in secret bold font,
While I chase after crumbs, of what I might want.
It whispers sweet nothings, quite out of sync,
I laugh at its antics, oh, what will I think?

In the quiet of evening, it starts to sway,
With the rhythms of crickets and the moonlight's play.
I join in the dance, with my slippers askew,
A silent duet, just my heart and a shoe.

With every heartbeat, a giggle's released,
In the chronicles swirling, the chaos increased.
The drama unfolds, as I snicker and grin,
My heart's little stories are where laughs begin.

So here's to the silence, where giggles abound,
In the depths of my chest, whimsy is found.
Together we frolic through pages so daft,
The unspoken saga, the funniest craft.

A Journey Through Quiet Spaces

In a room so still and neat,
I dance with shadows at my feet.
My socks do slide, my elbow hits,
The lamp that winks, my solitude fits.

The vacuum hums a gentle tune,
It's my friend beneath the moon.
I laugh with dust bunnies along the way,
We hold a party every Saturday.

The fridge's light is my spotlight,
It gleams on leftover bites tonight.
I juggle fruits, a banana here,
The kitchen's my stage, let's give a cheer!

With popcorn popped, I sit and wink,
Together we nibble, and then we think.
In quiet spaces, we find our groove,
A silly dance, who needs to move?

The Song of Silent Echoes

In silence, I find a funny beat,
With echoes dancing, oh so sweet.
I sing to cats, they just stare back,
A chorus of meows, what a lack!

A chair that creaks, it's tapping toes,
A rhythm born where no one goes.
I hum a tune, the dust motes sway,
Invisible friends join the play.

The clock ticks loud, a drummer's beat,
While mice in corners tap their feet.
I serenade each empty chair,
And they applaud, with nary a care.

With walls that listen and laugh along,
I write my quiet, silly song.
In the void where no voices meet,
I'm the queen of this quaint retreat.

Dreams Beneath the Stars

Under the stars, my dreams take flight,
A blanket of quiet, oh what delight!
I chat with crickets, they sing so loud,
About my day and make me proud.

The moon hears secrets in whispers bright,
As I ponder if ghosts eat at night.
A squirrel drops by, with plans to scheme,
He's plotting a heist for my ice cream.

The breeze joins in, it rustles the leaves,
Tickling my nose, oh how it deceives.
We giggle and laugh, of mischief and fun,
A starry night full of joy has begun.

A dream takes shape, I'm dancing on air,
With each twirl, it's beyond compare.
In shadows' embrace, my laughter blooms,
Painting the night with soft, silly tunes.

The Harmony of Being Alone

In cozy corners, I find my peace,
A solo act that will never cease.
With socks that clash, who needs a pair?
My style's unique, beyond compare.

The toaster pops, a breakfast cheer,
It's joined by coffee, my best dear.
Together we plot a morning jam,
With burnt toast songs, they taste like glam.

The chair reclines, it knows my woes,
A silent buddy, as tension flows.
We laugh at life and what it brings,
While serenading with funny flings.

In solitude's arms, I giggle and sway,
Creating joy in my own silly way.
In harmony found within my space,
I'm solo, but oh, it's a happy place!

Sheltered Among Shadows

In the corner, a chair sits tight,
Hiding secrets in the night.
A sock lies lonely on the floor,
It dreams of dancing, wanting more.

The fridge hums a merry tune,
While my plants plot a green monsoon.
A cat is napping on the bin,
Judging me for the snacks I've sin.

In the dark, my snacks await,
Cheesy puffs on a paper plate.
I chuckle at the quiet show,
Where shadows sway and laughter grows.

Alone but happy, I declare,
A party of one, I've got to share.
With ghosts of friends and laughter loud,
I'm the life of this silent crowd.

The Solitary Traveler's Song

A suitcase filled with socks and dreams,
I wander on, or so it seems.
The map says left, I take a right,
A twisty road, what a delight!

I spot a tree that's talking loud,
It tells my woes; I laugh out proud.
With every step, I trip and fall,
A solo dance, my every call.

A donut shop can cure all ills,
I munch my way through joy's good thrills.
The waiter knows me by my style,
He serves me smiles with every mile.

Yet on my way, I see a pair,
Two birds who smile without a care.
I mimic them, a silly spree,
In solitude, I jest with glee.

Whispered Wishes in the Silence

In a quiet nook, I wish on stars,
While counting all my silly scars.
The dust bunnies dance, a waltz so sweet,
No one's around to miss my feet.

A teapot whistles a lively tune,
It dreams of tea parties 'neath the moon.
I join in, a silly duet,
With every pour, my woes I forget.

The curtains sway like they're in a show,
I clap for them, they put on a glow.
In this hush, I hear my thoughts collide,
They giggle and roll, no need to hide.

I pull a blanket, wrap it tight,
In this cozy chaos, everything's right.
With whispers of wishes filling the air,
I'm best friends with silence; it's a lovely affair.

The Journey into Inner Wilderness

With a map that's drawn in crayon bright,
I set forth into my thoughts tonight.
The jungle's thick with thoughts that roam,
Each rustle leads me closer to home.

A squirrel gives me life advice,
He says to roll the dice, be nice.
I nod and ponder, make a face,
In this wild place, there's no time to race.

I navigate through dreams and fears,
Collecting giggles, drowning tears.
A cheesecake waits at the journey's end,
It's my steadfast, sugary friend.

In this wilderness, deep and wide,
I brave it all, with smiles as my guide.
The journey's fun, though I feel absurd,
In the land of whims, my heart is stirred.

Still Waters Run Deep

In a pond where frogs all croak,
The fish just think it's some strange joke.
A turtle sunbathes on a log,
While the catfish dances like a prog.

Bubbles rise with every splash,
The dragonfly thinks it's quite the bash.
While minnows gather round the edges,
The heron sneaks like quiet pledges.

But oh, the silence is quite grand,
Except for all these fishy bands.
They sing their tunes in watery realms,
With just a pinch of whimsy, please—no elves!

So let the waters play and sway,
While afternoon turns into play.
In this embrace, we find our stilts,
And laugh at life while making quilts.

Veils of Isolation

Behind my door, I choose to hide,
From the noisy world outside.
The cat's my friend, a trusty mate,
He listens well, no need to wait.

My socks are mismatched, it's quite the sight,
I wear them proud, and oh so light.
The pizza box is my best chair,
With sights and smells floating in the air.

Tea parties with my teddy bear,
He's a tad rude, but I don't care.
We sip our dreams from mugs so huge,
While crafting plans for socks that fuse.

Through curtains drawn, the sun peeks in,
To catch me grinning with my kin.
A world of silence, laughter, glee,
In my odd, quirky jubilee!

Beneath the Tranquil Canopy

Under the shade of leafy greens,
I spy on ants and their routines.
They march in lines with lots of zeal,
As I sit here munching on my meal.

The squirrels play tag, their acorn prize,
While I marvel at their crafty lies.
They think they rule the lofty trees,
But I have snacks to share with ease.

A gentle breeze tickles my nose,
Making me laugh in blissful prose.
A bird serenades from high above,
While I wave back from my nest of love.

So here I sit, in quiet mirth,
The best of all this loony earth.
With critters sharing this sweet escape,
Laughter echoes in this leafy drape.

The Forgotten Garden

In a garden filled with weeds and dust,
Daisies plot and laugh, they must.
The roses sigh with tangled hair,
While dandelions dance, unaware.

Gnomes stare idle, mossy and wise,
Judging me with their stone-cold eyes.
But in this chaos, jokes abound,
With plants that whisper, 'Let's stick around!'

Sunflowers sway in a funny trance,
Hoping for bees to join their dance.
A cabbage grins, its leaves like capes,
While beetles gossip of silly shapes.

Here I roam in muddy shoes,
With laughter echoing, I refuse.
To tidy up this quirky plot,
I'll leave it wild, like a jolly thought!

Untouched Corners of the Earth

In a corner where dust bunnies play,
A rubber chicken rests at bay.
The chairs hold meetings, quite absurd,
As crickets chirp, but do not speak a word.

The fridge hums secrets, old and stale,
While socks escape on their own trail.
A lonesome spoon dreams of a dance,
With empty bowls, it takes a chance.

Tube socks argue, who's the best?
While gnomes keep watch, too shy to jest.
A napkin whispers, "So bored, I sigh,"
As dust settles on a ketchup bottle nearby.

But in odd places, laughter hides,
The tickling tales of old shoe rides.
In little nooks, the giggles sprout,
In corners untouched, joy's about.

When Winds Embrace the Void

The wind whips wildly in empty halls,
A poltergeist spins, then suddenly stalls.
It tickles the curtains like a playful ghost,
While the vacuum cleaner mocks with a boast.

Balloons float high, all alone in the air,
While whispers of sneakers plot a new affair.
The door creaks open, then slams with glee,
Inviting the silence for tea, just for three.

A tumbleweed rolls, it whispers of fun,
While sunbeams chase shadows, just on the run.
The echo of laughter dances through space,
In this joyous void, all find their place.

Strange critters frolic in corners unseen,
While society's norm takes a break, so serene.
Winds swirl together, embracing the odd,
In emptiness found, they all applaud.

The Heart's Quiet Soliloquy

In isolation where echoes sigh,
A rubber band ponders way up high.
Heartbeats syncopate with a snore,
While lonely socks hold a silent score.

A teapot grumbles, longing for tea,
In the solitude of self, it starts to decree.
The cookie jar giggles, 'Come take a bite!'
While a spoon plays dipsy doodle in pure delight.

Silent whispers fill the empty halls,
An old piano faithfully recalls.
The shadows start waltzing, not quite shy,
Inviting the dust bunnies to say hi.

A heart speaks volumes in quiet prose,
While mismatched plates gossip without close.
In the stillness, laughter can grow,
In the serene, giggles flow.

Threads of Silence in a Tattered Fabric

Tattered threads weave with a laugh,
In the fabric of stillness, they draw a path.
Buttons giggle at the seams, quite bold,
As needles and yarn spin tales long told.

In cluttered boxes, dust meets thread,
While the quilt murmurs, "Are we all fed?"
The thimble teeters on a careless edge,
While twine ties secrets in laughter's hedge.

Old patterns dance in the cobwebbed light,
While scissors sharpen their wit, just right.
"Cut and sew!" they whisper with glee,
Creating a masterpiece for all to see.

Yet in each fold, a chuckle is found,
As the fabric of silence spins round and round.
In stitched-up corners, wild tales emerge,
Laughter and whispers begin to surge.

In the Company of Myself

I chat with my reflection, quite the talker,
A real comedian, all jokes and laughter.
We share a snack, then I would wager,
I'm the only one who'll ever judge my flavor.

Each thought a party, balloons in my head,
Dancing on my pillow, a confetti bed.
A silent cheerleader, I root for my plight,
But tripping on my thoughts gives me a fright!

I juggle my hopes like a circus act,
One falls, I just grin, that's how I reacted.
A clown with a nose, I wear all the hats,
No one but me sees the punchline in that!

So here I remain on this delightfully tightrope,
In laughter, I sway, with a smirk and a hope.
In the company of laughter, I rarely frown,
Making myself giggle won't bring me down.

The Nest of Longing

In a comfy cocoon where my thoughts like to play,
I count all my wishes, quite a feathery display.
With dreams on like slippers, I shuffle around,
The echo of silence, a whimsical sound.

Feathers of hope poke my slumbering mind,
Tickling my thoughts, they're gentle but blind.
I'd build a great nest with snacks piled so high,
And though it's just me, I'd still need a pie!

In this quirky abode, I nestle and puff,
Clutching my longing, cozy and tough.
I toss in some giggles, add in a tune,
A weird little ballet, my own private room.

So if you should wander and hear giggles galore,
Just know it's my longing, it's never a bore.
With a nest that's all mine, I'll never feel blue,
In a world that's my own, I make my debut.

Shadows Intertwined

A dance in the twilight, my shadow's a friend,
We twirl and we swirl till the daylight could bend.
With funny little steps, we shuffle about,
Two partners in crime, with a whispered shout.

It tickles and teases, a light-hearted jest,
As we wander the night, all dressed in our best.
We mime out our stories, with giggles we share,
Making silly poses, without a care.

On walls, we project our wild little dreams,
Dancing with caution down shimmering beams.
But when dawn arrives, like magic it fades,
Just me and my thoughts in the sunlight cascades.

Yet in the moonlight, our spirits take flight,
Crafting new adventures in the cloak of the night.
For shadows may leave, yet laughter stays found,
In the corners of silence where joy will abound.

The Silent Dance of Time

Tick-tock, the clock's got a wiggly groove,
Moves like a dancer with something to prove.
I watch as it strolls with a playful hum,
Each second a jig, not a single one glum.

It teases with moments, a peek-a-boo game,
Whispering softly, yet never quite tame.
I trip over memories, they laugh and they cheer,
Time throws its arms wide, no need for fear.

Each tick is a chuckle, a wink from the past,
As I gather my thoughts, they skitter quite fast.
I hoot with delight at this cheeky charade,
As moments pirouette in a grand masquerade.

So here I shall sit, watch the hours parade,
With laughter as currency, my worries delayed.
The silent dance swirls, and I'm part of the plot,
With giggles and grins, I embrace all I've got.

Within the Cavern of Thoughts

In my head, a circus spins,
Clowns trip over their own chins.
Thoughts are tangled, jumpy sprites,
Stealing snacks on sleepless nights.

I ponder life and what's my quest,
While socks fight back—it's all a jest.
Each memory's a silly dance,
In this funny mind, I take a chance.

In shadows cast by fleeting dreams,
I trip on laughter, or so it seems.
This winding path of giggles wide,
Leads me to where my quirks reside.

Echoes bounce in the empty hall,
As witty banter spins with gall.
In solitude, a jest unfolds,
A merry heart, despite the cold.

Raindrops on Solitary Leaves

Each drop a giggle, a tiny cheer,
Nature dances, without a care.
Leaves glide down like teetering hats,
Wearing droplets, like playful bats.

A robin hops, with a silly tune,
Singing loud as he dodges the swoon.
Wet feathers fluff in the splashing rain,
Raccoons smile amid the mundane.

In every puddle, reflections mend,
A wobbly ballet—no need to pretend.
The trees shake hands, their branches sway,
Each splash a slapstick play today.

Alone but not lonely, I rejoice,
In this laughter, I find my voice.
The sky fits snug in my quirky sleeve,
With nature's giggles—who needs reprieve?

The Void that Awakens

In silence deep, where echoes dream,
The void chuckles—it's not what it seems.
It juggles worries, tosses them high,
Yet wears a grin—oh, my, oh, my!

I sit and wonder what next to fear,
As the void whispers, 'Come talk to your beer.'
Thoughts take flight on a rollercoaster,
Whirling in circles, like a ghostly toaster.

Each whisper tickles, as shadows grow,
In the stillness, absurdities flow.
This emptiness, a frolicsome prank,
Turns worries into a parade—oh, thank!

Awakened by giggles, I find my way,
Through the void that leaps, a dance in the fray.
What lies beyond holds a comical hue,
Even in jest, I'm never blue.

Captured in Stillness

In the stillness of time, a misfit parade,
Resides my thoughts, in a curious charade.
Each moment a whoopee cushion, it seems,
Popping out laughter from slumbering dreams.

A chair creaks as if to partake,
In witty repartees that never forsake.
The clock winks, its hands on a spree,
Tick-tocking jokes, just to amuse me.

Solitude's corner is not quite bare,
For gnomes and giggles fill up the air.
Here silence has a very strange style,
Cracking wise like a mischievous smile.

Every pause dances, no need for a plan,
In stillness, I'm free—oh, what a fan!
Life's quirky charmer, in its silly twist,
Holds laughter's light—how could I resist?

Blossoms of the Unseen

In a garden where no one goes,
Dandelions dance in silent rows.
They laugh at weeds that try to thrive,
Unseen blooms are so alive!

A snail slides by, a careful creep,
While ants hold parties, secrets keep.
The flowers gossip, whispers sweet,
Wishing for guests, or just a treat!

Birds play chess in the empty air,
Forgetful of the world's loud glare.
A breeze rolls in with a chuckle,
Trading quiet for a little buckle!

So here I sit with thoughts so few,
Among the laughter no one knew.
These unseen blooms, they've got it right,
In their silly world, everything's bright!

Sifting Through the Quiet

In the hush, I find a sock,
It's been lost, like my other clock.
The quiet hum of dust on shelves,
Just me and my forgotten elves.

A spider spins a yarn of glue,
Shooting webs like thoughts untrue.
I sip my tea while ants debate,
Who'll reach the crumb, and who is late?

A shadow flits, I see it clear,
It's just my drink, I have no fear.
The whispers of the wind entice,
"Time for jokes, not once but twice!"

So here I dwell in silence deep,
With creeping thoughts that just won't sleep.
Sifting through dreams that come and go,
Finding chuckles in the flow!

The View from Within

Open my window to the great unknown,
A cat has seen it, all alone.
Through my glass, she makes a fuss,
While birds plot tales that make a plus!

Inside my mind, a circus plays,
With juggling thoughts and silly ways.
The view is bright, though quite absurd,
I'm the only one who's heard!

Umbrellas float like dreams on air,
While bubbles argue, "Life's unfair!"
I tip my hat to clouds that swoon,
And dance with shadows, late in June.

The world outside can search for gold,
But inside here, I'm never old.
The view from within, a funny sight,
With giggles echoing through the night!

The Tides of Isolation

Waves crash softly on the shore,
Seagulls squawk, they want some more.
While fish are busy playing hide,
A crab walks sideways, full of pride!

The jellyfish, they float and bounce,
In quiet depths, they twist and flounce.
A clam just sits, a rock in place,
"Why rush?" it muses, "At my pace!"

Shells gossip loudly, full of tales,
About the crab who never fails.
With each tide, a funny turn,
In isolation, still we learn!

So here I stand with sand to keep,
Among the waves, I laugh, I leap.
In tides of time, I hum my tune,
Isolation feels like a grand festoon!

Reflections in a Quiet Stream

There once was a frog in a pond,
Who croaked with a voice very fond.
He sang all alone,
To his reflection, a clone.

With a splash, he did leap and respond,
Thinking fish were just waiting to bond.
But they swam away fast,
His fame couldn't last.

So he puffed up his cheeks, then he'd yawn,
In his solitude's glow, he was drawn.
No chorus around,
Just his echo profound.

In his kingdom of lilly and light,
He danced with great glee, what a sight!
Though friends were all shy,
He'd still wave them goodbye.

The Essence of Being Alone

A cactus once wished for a hug,
But the desert just gave it a shrug.
With each prickly stare,
It thought, 'It's not fair!'

It adorned itself with a cap,
Wishing for a social map.
But gatherings fail,
Without friends, it's pale.

The sands whispered tales by the mile,
As the cactus just thirsted awhile.
No laughter was found,
Just the creaky ground.

With thoughts of a birthday parade,
The flowers all looked so dismayed.
Yet it waved with delight,
In its prickly respite.

Solitary Blossoms

In a garden where daisies all thrived,
One little bloom felt deprived.
With petals so bright,
But alone in the night.

It watched all the bees swoop and dive,
While wishing for someone to jive.
But the bees had their crew,
And left it on cue.

So it danced with the wind in its glee,
Creating grand visions of spree.
A flower in trance,
With the moon for a dance.

In solitude's shimmered embrace,
It twirled with great flair in its place.
Though alone it would bloom,
It found joy in the room.

The Lonesome Horizon

At dawn in the hills, oh so stark,
Stood a lone tree, quite a quirk.
It scratched at the sky,
With a big, leafy sigh.

No birds on its branches, so bare,
Just a wind that forgot to care.
As it stood there so proud,
In identity shroud.

But the clouds floated low with a tease,
Whispering sweet nothings like breeze.
With a giggle so soft,
They scooted aloft.

The sun rolled high with a grin,
As the tree rocked, tapping its shin.
All alone yet so free,
In the fun of the spree.

www.ingramcontent.com/pod-product-compliance
Lightning Source LLC
Chambersburg PA
CBHW070333120526
44590CB00017B/2870